WALT DISNEY
WORLD

BY MARNE VENTURA

CONTENT CONSULTANT
Sarah Nilsen, PhD
Associate Professor, Film and Television Studies
University of Vermont

Core Library

An Imprint of Abdo Publishing
abdobooks.com

Cover image: A statue in Walt Disney World honors
Walt Disney and his cartoon character Mickey Mouse.

abdobooks.com

Published by Abdo Publishing, a division of ABDO, PO Box 398166,
Minneapolis, Minnesota 55439. Copyright © 2020 by Abdo Consulting
Group, Inc. International copyrights reserved in all countries. No part of this
book may be reproduced in any form without written permission from the
publisher. Core Library™ is a trademark and logo of Abdo Publishing.

Printed in the United States of America, North Mankato, Minnesota
092019
012020

THIS BOOK CONTAINS
RECYCLED MATERIALS

Cover Photo: Michael Orso/Moment/Getty Images
Interior Photos: Michael Orso/Moment/Getty Images, 1; Gene Lester/Archive Photos/Getty
Images, 4–5; AP Images, 6, 15, 20–21, 26, 31, 43; Red Line Editorial, 9; John Raoux/AP Images,
10; Bill Grant/Alamy, 12–13; Fred Noel/AP Images, 24–25; Blaine Harrington III/Alamy, 28–29;
V. Filimonov/Shutterstock Images, 35 (camera); Vector Plotnikoff/Shutterstock Images, 35
(hamburger), 35 (hot dog), 35 (French fries); Shutterstock Images, 35 (popcorn); David Roark/Disney
Parks/Getty Images Entertainment/Getty Images, 36–37, 45

Editor: Maddie Spalding
Series Designer: Claire Vanden Branden

Library of Congress Control Number: 2019942367

Publisher's Cataloging-in-Publication Data

Names: Ventura, Marne, author.
Title: Walt Disney World / by Marne Ventura
Description: Minneapolis, Minnesota : Abdo Publishing, 2020 | Series: Iconic America | Includes
      online resources and index.
Identifiers: ISBN 9781532190957 (lib. bdg.) | ISBN 9781532176807 (ebook)
Subjects: LCSH: Walt Disney World (Fla.)--Juvenile literature. | Magic Kingdom (Fla.)--Juvenile
      literature. | Amusement parks--Florida--Juvenile literature. | Disney characters--Juvenile
      literature. | Theme parks--Juvenile literature.
Classification: DDC 917.5924--dc23

CONTENTS

A MAGICAL PLACE

Walt Disney sat on a miniature train in his backyard in Los Angeles, California. His two young daughters rode on the train cars behind him. They laughed and waved as the train chugged along the track.

Walt was a cartoonist and filmmaker. He had grown up around trains. His father and uncle worked on the railroad. As a teenager, Walt sold snacks and magazines to train passengers in Kansas City, Missouri. Walt later created one of his best-known characters on a

Walt Disney, *far left*, built railroad tracks and a miniature train in the backyard of his Los Angeles home.

Walt poses with his wife, Lillian, *left*, and their two daughters in 1949.

train ride. He came up with the idea for Mickey Mouse while traveling from New York to California in 1928.

Walt always kept a model train in his studio in Burbank, California. Many of his cartoon films included trains. After returning from the Chicago Railroad Fair in 1948, he decided to build his own backyard train. It was one-eighth of the size of a real train. He named the train the *Lilly Belle* after his wife, Lillian. He sometimes invited over his employees at Walt Disney Studios to ride the train too.

Walt spent Saturdays playing with his daughters. He took them to amusement parks or merry-go-rounds. These parks often disappointed Walt. Many were dirty and not well maintained. Walt wanted to create a safe and fun park for children and families. He came up with the idea for Mickey Mouse Park. He envisioned

DISNEY WORLD'S RAILROAD

In the 1960s, Walt had an idea for a park in Florida. The park became Walt Disney World. Walt wanted trains to transport visitors around the park. He hired mechanical engineer Roger Broggie. Broggie found four rusty train engines in Mexico. He bought them and had them sent to Florida. The engines were restored. They were named the Walter E. Disney, the Lilly Belle, the Roger E. Broggie, and the Roy O. Disney. Walt Disney World's railroad is the largest in Florida. More than 3 million people ride on the park's trains each year.

a train circling the park. This park later became Disneyland.

WALT'S PARKS

Disneyland opened in Anaheim, California, on July 17, 1955. Disneyland was a great success. So Walt began planning a second park near Orlando, Florida. The park opened on October 1, 1971. This park was called Walt Disney World Resort. Today it includes four theme parks: the Magic Kingdom Park, Epcot, Disney's Hollywood Studios, and Disney's Animal Kingdom. It has two water

DISNEY WORLD
VISITORS

This graph shows the number of people who visited Walt Disney World's four theme parks in 2018. Which theme park appears to be most popular? Does this graph help you better understand Walt Disney World's influence? Why or why not?

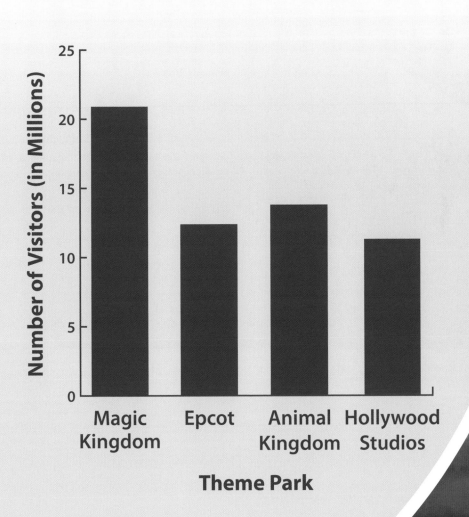

Number of Visitors (in Millions)

Theme Park

Magic Kingdom · Epcot · Animal Kingdom · Hollywood Studios

The Expedition Everest roller coaster in Animal Kingdom features a structure that looks like Mount Everest.

parks and 27,000 hotel rooms. It also has more than 300 restaurants and 300 shops. There are four golf courses and a sports complex.

Walt passed away in 1966, before construction on Walt Disney World began. Led by his older brother Roy Disney, a team of engineers and storytellers known as Imagineers kept working to create Walt Disney World. This fun and colorful resort is an important part of Walt's legacy. It is a place where guests of all ages can relax and play. For this reason, many people call Walt Disney World "The Most Magical Place on Earth."

FURTHER EVIDENCE

Chapter One discusses Walt's love of trains. What was one of the chapter's main points? What key evidence supports this point? Read the article at the website below. Does the information on the website support the point you identified? Does it present new evidence?

I HAVE ALWAYS LOVED TRAINS

abdocorelibrary.com/walt-disney-world

WALT DISNEY AND DISNEYLAND

Walter Elias Disney was born on December 5, 1901, in Chicago, Illinois. He had three older brothers and a younger sister. His mother, Flora, was a schoolteacher. His father, Elias, was a farmer and carpenter. When Walt was still a baby, the family moved to a farm in Missouri near the small town of Marceline. Walt started school in Marceline. He loved drawing and painting.

After a few years, Elias moved the family to Kansas City, Missouri. Walt was nine years

The Walt Disney Hometown Museum in Marceline, Missouri, shares the history of Walt's childhood and family life.

old at the time. Elias bought a newspaper route. Walt and his brothers had to get up early each morning to deliver papers before school. During this time, Walt enrolled in an art class. He studied cartooning. He later took classes at the Kansas City Art Institute and School of Design.

In 1917, Elias moved the family back to Chicago. At that time, Walt was 16 years old. He took photographs and made drawings for his high school's newspaper.

WORLD WAR I

By 1918, Walt's two older brothers had joined the US military to fight in World War I (1914–1918). Walt wanted to join too. He was interested in the US Navy. But he was still 16 years old at the time. He needed to be at least 18 years old to join the navy. The American Red Cross had a lower age requirement. People had to be at least 17 years old to join. So Walt decided to become a Red Cross ambulance driver. His mother signed a form that gave him permission to join.

Red Cross ambulance drivers prepare to receive wounded soldiers in England during World War I.

Walt changed his birth year on his passport application to 1900. He made himself appear one year older so he could join.

During the war, Walt drove an ambulance in France and Germany. He served overseas for 11 months. When he was not driving or repairing an ambulance, he spent his time drawing in his sketchbook.

EARLY CAREER

After the war ended, Walt returned to Kansas City. He began working as an artist-in-training in 1919. He drew artwork for advertisements on theater programs and catalogs. In the course of his work, he met another young artist named Ub Iwerks.

In 1922, Walt and Iwerks opened a film studio in Kansas City. They called it the Laugh-O-Gram Studio. They hired animators. Walt and his team made cartoon ads based on fairy tales and fables. These ads were shown at local movie theaters. Walt and his team also made a film called *Alice in Cartoonland.* This film had a cartoon background, but a real child actor played the main character, Alice. The film became widely popular.

Despite the success of *Alice in Cartoonland,* Walt's studio was losing money. In 1923, Walt decided to move to Los Angeles and open a new film studio with his brother Roy. They called their company the Disney Brothers Cartoon Studio.

SUCCESS

In 1926, the Disney brothers changed the name of their company to Walt Disney Studios. Walt's coworkers from Kansas City joined the company.

In 1928, Walt came up with the cartoon character Mickey Mouse. At this time, Walt Disney Studios was one of the first companies to add sound to animated films. Walt's company created a cartoon called *Steamboat Willie.* It featured Mickey Mouse and his girlfriend, Minnie Mouse. It had a soundtrack with sound effects and music. It was a huge success. Soon the company's team of animators invented other characters. These included Donald Duck, Pluto, and Goofy.

Walt's company became known as Walt Disney Productions in 1929. In 1932, Walt

ROY AND WALT

Roy was eight years older than Walt. Roy was protective of his brother. When they were younger, Roy had pushed baby Walt around in a stroller. Walt admired his big brother. Walt was the creative one. Roy was a good businessman. Sometimes they argued. Roy often tried to stop Walt from spending too much money or taking too many risks. But Roy's goal was to help Walt turn his ideas into reality. He valued Walt's creativity.

THE THREE LITTLE PIGS

The 1930s was a time of high unemployment. Many people could not find jobs. They struggled to make a living. This difficult period was called the Great Depression. In 1933, Walt Disney Productions released a new film called *The Three Little Pigs*. This cartoon appealed to many Americans. In the film, the pigs sing a song called "Who's Afraid of the Big Bad Wolf?" It became a song of hope for millions of people. To viewers, the pigs were a symbol of strength. People's spirits were uplifted when they saw how the pigs overcame their fears. This inspired Americans to face their own fears.

became one of the first filmmakers to add color to his films. Walt's earlier films had been in black and white.

Throughout the 1930s, Walt's company made cartoon movies that are still popular today. *Snow White and the Seven Dwarfs* came out in 1937. *Pinocchio*, *Dumbo*, and *Bambi* followed. By 1940, Walt's company had grown so much that he had to move to a bigger studio in Burbank.

DISNEYLAND

In the early 1950s, Walt decided to build a big amusement park in Anaheim, California. He called the park Disneyland. It was made up of five parts: Main Street, Fantasyland, Adventureland, Frontierland, and Tomorrowland. Main Street was modeled after the town of Marceline. Fantasyland, Adventureland, Frontierland, and Tomorrowland were themed lands. The Disneyland park opened in 1955 after one year of construction.

EXPLORE ONLINE

Chapter Two talks about Walt's childhood and family life. The article at the website below gives more information about Walt's background. What new information did you learn from the website?

WALT DISNEY
abdocorelibrary.com/walt-disney-world

MAKING IT BETTER

When Walt built Disneyland, it was surrounded by orange groves. There were no nearby buildings. But the park became so popular that people soon opened businesses nearby. By late 1958, restaurants and motels had been built around the park. More and more visitors came to Disneyland. Despite this rising popularity, Walt had some concerns. Walt could not control the quality of these businesses. Walt Disney Productions also did not get any money from these businesses.

Crowds of people rushed to the entrance of Fantasyland in Disneyland when the park first opened on July 17, 1955.

Traffic jams were common when Disneyland opened and closed each day. Walt wanted to make a bigger, better Disneyland. He wanted guests to be able to come and go easily. He also wanted to have more control over surrounding businesses. He planned to create a "city of the future." It would feature new inventions. People would be able to live and work there.

PROJECT X

Walt spent five years looking for a place to build. He needed lots of land and good weather year-round. In 1963, Walt flew over Florida to explore potential locations for his new park. He saw vast wetlands in the middle of the state. Two main highways were being built there. An airport was nearby. Walt decided this would be the spot for his second park.

A WORLDWIDE INFLUENCE

Walt's vision led to the creation of 12 Disney theme parks worldwide. The four in Florida are the Magic Kingdom, Hollywood Studios, Epcot, and the Animal Kingdom. These four theme parks are part of Walt Disney World. There are two Disney theme parks in California. They are Disneyland and California Adventure. Tokyo, Japan, has a Disneyland park and a park called DisneySea. There is a Disneyland in Paris, France, too. Another Disney park in Paris is called Walt Disney Studios Park. There are also Disneyland parks in Hong Kong and Shanghai, China.

The land Walt wanted to build the park on was cheap. But he predicted that landowners would

Walt, *left*, and his brother Roy, *far right*, held a press conference in Orlando in November 1965 to discuss their plans for Walt Disney World.

raise the price of the land if they discovered he was the buyer. So Walt and his coworkers started new companies. They gave the companies code names such as Retlaw and M. T. Lott. Retlaw was "Walter" spelled backwards, and M. T. Lott was a code name for "Empty Lot."

Walt called the secret plan to build his second park "Project X." He was able to keep the project secret for

a while. But soon local workers and reporters became suspicious. They wondered who was buying so much land and why. Eventually, a reporter for the newspaper the *Orlando Sentinel* guessed that Walt was the buyer. In 1965, she wrote a story for the newspaper and shared her prediction. By that time, Walt had bought more than 27,000 acres (10,926 ha) for his new park.

In November 1965, Walt, Roy, and the governor of Florida announced the news. Walt and his Imagineers

It took workers approximately 18 months to build Cinderella's Castle at Walt Disney World.

then began planning the new park. Builders started to prepare the land. But on December 15, 1966, Walt died of lung cancer. His brother Roy had been about to retire. Instead he got to work. He turned Walt Disney World, his brother's dream, into reality.

STRAIGHT TO THE
SOURCE

In 1956, Walt spoke with a journalist about Disneyland.
He said:

> *The park means a lot to me in that it's something that will never be finished. Something that I can keep developing, keep . . . adding to—it's alive. It will be a live, breathing thing that will need changes. A picture is a thing that once you wrap it up . . . you're through . . . I wanted something live, something that could grow. . . . The park is that. Not only can I add things but even the trees will keep growing; the thing will get more beautiful every year.*

> Source: Walt Disney. "In Walt's Own Words: Plussing Disneyland." *The Walt Disney Family Museum Blog*. The Walt Disney Family Museum, July 17, 2014. Web. Accessed June 18, 2019.

What's the Big Idea?
Read the quote from Walt Disney carefully. Why was building a park important to Walt? What was his vision for his parks?

BUILDING DISNEY WORLD

The construction of Walt Disney World was a difficult process. Walt Disney Productions drained some wetlands in central Florida. Workers built miles of drainage canals. They created a lake called the Seven Seas Lagoon. The soil dug up to create this lake was spread out to raise the ground level of the park. This was done to prevent flooding. Construction crews then created a hidden, underground floor. The parts of the park that are visible to guests are called onstage. Hidden places are called backstage.

Performers sing and dance on Main Street, USA, in Walt Disney World.

When guests enter the park, they are on the second level. Many people who work at Walt Disney World are performers. They dress up in costumes. They look and act like Disney characters. Performers use underground tunnels to enter and exit the park, change costumes, or take a break without being seen.

ATTRACTIONS

Walt Disney World was designed to look similar to Disneyland. Workers built two hotels, a campground, and a theme park

Walt Disney World performers dressed as Disney characters for a 1971 parade.

called Magic Kingdom. They created a monorail to carry visitors across the park.

Walt Disney World opened on October 1, 1971. More than 10,000 guests came. Performers dressed as

Mickey Mouse, Donald Duck, Pluto, and Goofy greeted them. The resort's dedication ceremony happened later, on October 25. Roy Disney gave an inspiring speech.

People were drawn to the many attractions at Magic Kingdom. One main attraction was Cinderella's Castle. The 189-foot (58-m) tall castle gets gradually thinner from the bottom to the top. This makes it look taller than it actually is. Other original attractions included Snow White's Adventures and 20,000 Leagues Under the Sea. These were rides. Snow White's Adventures featured characters from the 1937 Disney movie *Snow White and the Seven Dwarves*. The 20,000 Leagues Under the Sea ride gave people the experience of being underwater in a submarine.

CHANGES AND ADDITIONS

On December 20, 1971, Roy died from lung cancer. He was 78 years old. Members of Walt Disney Productions tried to decide who would run the company. No one person was prepared to take on the leadership role.

This threatened the survival of the company. The company struggled for a time, but eventually recovered.

In 1982, Epcot opened. This theme park within Walt Disney World is made up of two parts. One part is called Future World, where visitors can try out new technologies. The other part is called World Showcase.

World Showcase is built around a lagoon. Buildings that represent 11 different countries circle the lagoon. Visitors get a feel for each country's architecture, foods, and cultures.

THE WORLD SHOWCASE

Walt Disney Productions modeled the World Showcase after a world's fair. A world's fair is an event where items from all over the world are displayed. Walt had created some attractions for the 1964 New York World's Fair. These attractions included a boat ride called It's a Small World, a car ride called Ford's Magic Skyway, and a show with a robot of President Abraham Lincoln. These World Fair attractions were later moved to the Disney parks. The Lincoln robot became part of the Hall of Presidents ride.

In 1989, Disney-MGM Studios was added to Walt Disney World. It was a TV and movie production studio. It later also became a theme park. Today, this theme park is called Disney's Hollywood Studios.

Other major additions were also made to Walt Disney World in 1989. Walt Disney World's first luxury resort was built that year. Four more hotels were completed. The Typhoon Lagoon Water Park opened.

By 1990, 500 million people visited Walt Disney World each year. By then, the name of Walt's company had changed. It was called the Walt Disney Company. In January, company chairperson Michael D. Eisner announced a plan. The plan was called the Disney Decade because it was a ten-year plan. It included the building of Animal Kingdom, a park with animal-themed rides and attractions. Animal Kingdom became the fourth Walt Disney World theme park when it opened in 1998.

FUN
FACTS

This graphic shares some interesting facts about Walt Disney World. What do these facts tell you about the resort and its size?

 Disney photographers take between 100,000 and 200,000 photos of guests each day.

 Guests eat 10 million hamburgers each year.

 Guests eat 6 million hot dogs each year.

 Guests eat 9 million pounds (4 million kg) of French fries each year.

 Guests eat more than 300,000 pounds (136,000 kg) of popcorn each year.

CHAPTER
FIVE

DISNEY WORLD TODAY

Today, Walt Disney World has made Florida an international tourist destination. The resort is open every day. Approximately 70,000 people work at Walt Disney World.

The Walt Disney Company has purchased other companies since the 1990s. For example, the company bought Lucasfilm in 2012. This film company created the Star Wars movies. In 2019, the Walt Disney Company purchased 20th Century Fox. This film company had made the movie *Avatar*. As a result, the Walt Disney

At Disney World, people can visit Star Wars Launch Bay to see real costumes, movie props, and more from the films.

Company has been able to create a greater variety of theme park attractions. In 2017, a new themed area opened in Disney's Animal Kingdom. It is called Pandora – The World of *Avatar*. This area looks like the setting in *Avatar*. A Star Wars–themed area was added to Hollywood Studios in 2019.

New technologies will be showcased in Walt Disney World in the future. One promising technology is a new type of robot Disney calls Stuntronics. Imagineers are designing these lifelike robots. The robots will be able to do superhero stunts such as flying. They could be used as stunt doubles for performers in the park.

EVERYONE IS WELCOME

The Walt Disney Company is widely known for its inclusion and fair hiring practices. The company hires people of many different cultures and backgrounds. It was one of the first companies to give employment benefits to LGBTQ employees. The company works to make it easy for people with disabilities to move about the park.

AN ECO-FRIENDLY COMPANY

The Walt Disney Company aims to make Walt Disney World resort eco-friendly. This means the company tries to reduce the resort's impact on the environment. In 1995, the Walt Disney Company created the Disney Conservation Fund. The fund supports projects to protect wildlife around the world. It has given more than $70 million to such projects. At Animal Kingdom, kids can learn about the destruction of wildlife habitats. Walt Disney Studios also creates films called Disneynature that educate viewers about wildlife.

In 2016, the Walt Disney Company created a 22-acre (9-ha) solar energy array. It is in the shape of a giant Mickey Mouse head. It converts sunlight to energy. The energy is used to power some of the park's attractions. Then in 2019, the company created a 270-acre (110-ha) solar farm near Animal Kingdom.

Walt Disney World is eco-friendly in other ways too. The resort uses fuel made from cooking oil and food waste in its buses. When employees light up Cinderella's Castle for the holidays, they use 170,000 LED lights. LED lights use less energy than traditional lighting.

WALT'S LEGACY

Walt's idea was to create a magical place for families everywhere. His vision led to the creation of the resort where his characters come to life. Walt is remembered for his creativity and enthusiasm. Walt Disney World Resort is part of his impressive legacy.

STRAIGHT TO THE
SOURCE

Marty Sklar became the Imagineering creative director in 1974. He worked for the Walt Disney Company for more than 50 years. He wrote scripts and helped Walt develop theme parks. In a 2013 interview, Sklar spoke about his work:

> There are two ways to look at a blank piece of paper. One way is it's the most frightening thing in the world because you have to make the first mark on it. The way we taught the Imagineers to think about that blank page is it's the greatest opportunity in the world. Because you GET to make the first mark on that page and let your imagination fly. It was a wonderful opportunity for all of us, and the greatest influence in my career.

> Source: Dave Parfitt. "Interview with Walt Disney Imagineering Legend Marty Sklar on Creating Magic Kingdoms." *Adventures by Daddy*. Adventures by Daddy, July 12, 2013. Web. Accessed July 15, 2019.

Consider Your Audience

Adapt this passage for a different audience, such as your friends. Write a blog post conveying this same information for the new audience. How does your post differ from the original text and why?

IMPORTANT
DATES

1901
Walter Elias Disney is born in Chicago, Illinois, on December 5.

1923
Walt opens a cartoon studio with his brother Roy in Los Angeles, California.

1928
Walt creates the cartoon character Mickey Mouse.

1955
Disneyland opens in Anaheim, California, on July 17.

1966
Walt dies of lung cancer on December 15.

1971
Walt Disney World Resort opens in Orlando, Florida, on October 1.

1982
Epcot opens.

1998
Animal Kingdom opens.

2017
Pandora opens in Animal Kingdom.

2019
A Star Wars area opens in Hollywood Studios.

STOP AND
THINK

Tell the Tale

Chapter Two discusses some of the Walt Disney Company's early cartoons. Imagine you were visiting Walt's studio in the 1920s or 1930s. Write 200 words about what you see at the studio. What are some cartoon characters you might see?

Dig Deeper

After reading this book, what questions do you still have about Walt Disney World? With an adult's help, find a few reliable sources that can help you answer your questions. Write a paragraph about what you learned.

Take a Stand

The Walt Disney Company works to make its parks eco-friendly. Do you think its efforts are enough? Or do you think the company could do more to accomplish this goal? Why is it important for large parks and resorts such as Walt Disney World to be eco-friendly?

You Are There

This book discusses the opening day of Walt Disney World. Imagine you were there when the park opened. Write a letter home telling your friends what you saw. What rides and attractions did you go on? Be sure to add plenty of details to your letter.

GLOSSARY

animator
someone who creates
cartoons for motion pictures

array
a large group of things that
are organized into rows
or columns

canal
a manmade waterway that
is used for travel and that
distributes water

grove
a small stand of trees

lagoon
a shallow manmade pond or
lake that connects to a larger
body of water

LGBTQ
a term that stands for
lesbian, gay, bisexual,
transgender, and queer
or questioning

modeled
based on

monorail
a car or train that runs on a
single track

resort
a place to stay for fun

soundtrack
music and other sounds that
accompany a motion picture

wetland
an area of land covered with
shallow water

ONLINE RESOURCES

To learn more about Walt Disney World, visit our free resource websites below.

Visit **abdocorelibrary.com** or scan this QR code for free Common Core resources for teachers and students, including vetted activities, multimedia, and booklinks, for deeper subject comprehension.

Visit **abdobooklinks.com** or scan this QR code for free additional online weblinks for further learning. These links are routinely monitored and updated to provide the most current information available.

LEARN MORE

Hamilton, John. *Florida: The Sunshine State*. Minneapolis, MN: Abdo Publishing, 2017.

Holub, Joan. *Where Is Walt Disney World?* New York: Penguin Workshop, 2018.

INDEX

About the Author

Marne Ventura has written more than 100 books for children. A former elementary school teacher, she holds a master's degree in education from the University of California. Her favorite subjects are history, science, food, arts and crafts, and the lives of creative people. Marne and her husband live on the central coast of California.